EXPLORING COUNTRIES

Nigeria

by Lisa Owings

BELLWETHER MEDIA · MINNEAPOLIS, MN

Note to Librarians, Teachers, and Parents:

Blastoff! Readers are carefully developed by literacy experts and combine standards-based content with developmentally appropriate text.

Level 1 provides the most support through repetition of high-frequency words, light text, predictable sentence patterns, and strong visual support.

Level 2 offers early readers a bit more challenge through varied simple sentences, increased text load, and less repetition of high-frequency words.

Level 3 advances early-fluent readers toward fluency through increased text and concept load, less reliance on visuals, longer sentences, and more literary language.

Level 4 builds reading stamina by providing more text per page, increased use of punctuation, greater variation in sentence patterns, and increasingly challenging vocabulary.

Level 5 encourages children to move from "learning to read" to "reading to learn" by providing even more text, varied writing styles, and less familiar topics.

Whichever book is right for your reader, Blastoff! Readers are the perfect books to build confidence and encourage a love of reading that will last a lifetime!

This edition first published in 2012 by Bellwether Media, Inc.

No part of this publication may be reproduced in whole or in part without written permission of the publisher. For information regarding permission, write to Bellwether Media, Inc., Attention: Permissions Department, 5357 Penn Avenue South, Minneapolis, MN 55419.

Library of Congress Cataloging-in-Publication Data
Owings, Lisa.
 Nigeria / by Lisa Owings.
   p. cm. – (Blastoff! readers) (Exploring countries)
 Summary: "Developed by literacy experts for students in grades three through seven, this book introduces young readers to the geography and culture of Nigeria"–Provided by publisher.
 Includes bibliographical references and index.
 ISBN-13: 978-1-60014-619-0 (hardcover : alk. paper)
 ISBN-10: 1-60014-619-8 (hardcover : alk. paper)
 1. Nigeria–Juvenile literature. I. Title.
DT515.22.O975 2011
966.9–dc22   2011002229

Printed in the United States of America, North Mankato, MN.

080111   1187

Contents

Niger

Benin

Nigeria

Abuja ★

Gulf
of
Guinea

Cameroon

Did you know?
The Cameroon Highlands rise along Nigeria's border with Cameroon. Their tallest peak is Chappal Waddi. At 7,936 feet (2,419 meters), it is the highest point in Nigeria.

Chad

Nigeria is a country on the western coast of Africa. It spans 356,669 square miles (923,768 square kilometers) of the **continent**. Nigeria's southern shore lies along the **Gulf** of Guinea. The rest of the country is surrounded by land. Nigeria shares borders with Benin to the west, Niger to the north, and Cameroon to the east. Its northeastern corner touches Chad. Abuja is the capital of Nigeria. It was chosen for its location near the center of the country.

savannah

Nigeria's warm climate supports several different **biomes**. Most of northern Nigeria is covered in **savannahs**. Only a few trees and shrubs can grow in these dry grasslands. Southern Nigeria is wet enough for **tropical rain forests** to grow. Near the coast, the rain forests thin out into freshwater swamps and **mangrove forests**.

The rocky Jos **Plateau** rises in the center of Nigeria. Rivers and waterfalls flow down its steep slopes. South of the plateau, the Benue River flows from the east to join the Niger River in the west. The mighty Niger River then continues south and empties into the Gulf of Guinea. The Niger **Delta** lies where the river meets the gulf.

Did you know?

Lake Chad occupies the northeastern corner of the country. Nigeria shares this shallow lake with Chad, Niger, and Cameroon. The lake's size changes depending on the annual rainfall.

Lake Chad

Mangrove Forests

Did you know?

Some mangrove trees have roots that grow up from the sea floor and poke above the water. These roots help the trees breathe.

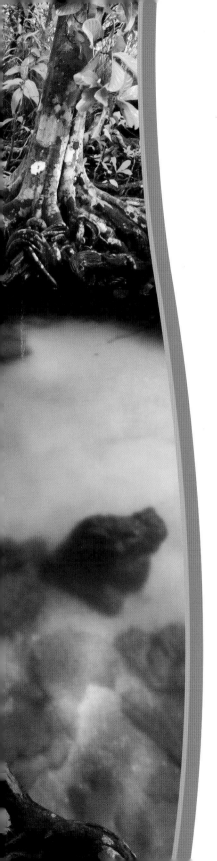

Nigeria has the largest area of mangrove forests in Africa. Mangrove trees grow in the salty water along the coast. Their unique roots let them survive in this environment. Mangrove roots act like stilts to lift the trees above the water. They **filter** salt from the water and absorb air through tiny holes in their bark.

Mangrove forests help keep Nigeria's coast healthy. They protect the shore from storms and ocean waves. Their tangled roots hold mud together to prevent **erosion**. The calm waters of mangrove forests also provide a safe home for sea creatures small enough to swim among the roots.

black crowned crane

Did you know?
National parks protect Nigeria's wildlife from habitat loss and hunting. Many animals find safe homes in Yankari, Gashaka Gumti, and Cross River National Parks.

Each biome in Nigeria is home to different kinds of animals. Lions and cheetahs stalk antelope, impala, and other animals on the savannah. Giraffes graze on the savannah's trees and grasses. The black crowned crane, Nigeria's national bird, flies above.

gorilla

giraffes

pangolin

The rain forest provides shelter for African forest elephants,
giant forest hogs, African golden cats, and chimpanzees.
Hercules baboon tarantulas creep along the rain forest
floor. In the mountains, gorillas roam around eating plants
and roots. Crocodiles and hippopotamuses lurk in the
country's **wetlands** and rivers. They share their watery
homes with manatees, turtles, crabs, and fish.

fun fact

The areas in which the Hausa-Fulani, Yoruba, and Igbo live are often called Hausaland, Yorubaland, and Igboland.

More people live in Nigeria than in any other country in Africa. Over 152 million people call it home. Nigeria is known for its **diversity**. Around 250 different people groups live throughout the country. The three largest are the Hausa-Fulani, the Yoruba, and the Igbo. About 3 out of every 10 Nigerians are Hausa-Fulani. They live in northern Nigeria. The Igbo and the Yoruba live in the southern half of the country. Smaller groups include the Ijaw, Kanuri, Ibibio, and Tiv. Many groups have their own traditions, religions, and languages. The most common African languages are Hausa, Yoruba, and Igbo. English is the official language of Nigeria.

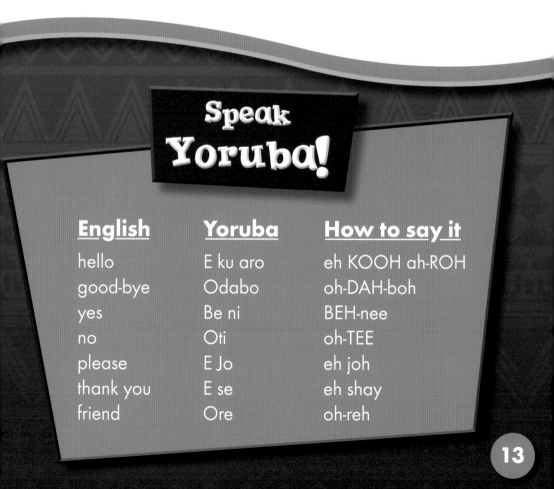

Speak Yoruba!

English	Yoruba	How to say it
hello	E ku aro	eh KOOH ah-ROH
good-bye	Odabo	oh-DAH-boh
yes	Be ni	BEH-nee
no	Oti	oh-TEE
please	E Jo	eh joh
thank you	E se	eh shay
friend	Ore	oh-reh

Did you know?

Some cities in Nigeria are so crowded that there is not enough electricity for everyone. Power outages are a normal part of life.

About half of all Nigerians live in cities. Most families have apartments or houses. Some live in crowded **slums**. City streets are packed with cars, motorcycles, and taxis. Women walk to and from the town market with large bundles of goods on their heads. Most people find everything they need at the market.

Life in Nigeria's countryside has changed little over hundreds of years. Families live close to each other in small groups of houses. The houses are built around an open area where people cook and play. Everyone helps with chores. They walk or share cars when they need to travel to other villages or towns. The market is the center of every village.

Where People Live in Nigeria

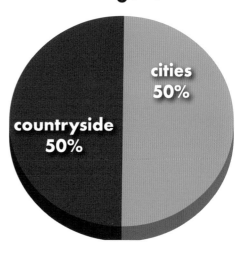

cities 50%

countryside 50%

fun fact

Most houses in Nigeria's countryside are made of mud. Grasses, leaves, or sheets of metal can be used for the roof.

Children in Nigeria are required to attend school from ages 6 to 15. Elementary school lasts for six years. Children study English and the African languages spoken in their area. They also learn science and math.

After elementary school, students attend three years of middle school. They add social studies, art, and music to their studies. Middle school students must pass an exam to get into high school. Nigerians who graduate from high school can attend one of the country's more than 50 universities.

Did you know?

Many Nigerians create their own jobs. In outdoor markets, they sell homegrown food or handmade goods like soap, pottery, and woven mats.

Where People Work in Nigeria

farming 70%

services 20%

manufacturing 10%

Most Nigerians in the countryside are farmers. They grow grains, peanuts, and cotton in the dry northern plains. In the south, the most important crops are **tubers** like taro, cassava, and yams. Some farmers raise cattle, sheep, goats, and pigs. Nigerians also get many **natural resources** from the earth. Workers drill for oil in the Niger Delta. Miners dig for tin in the Jos Plateau.

Workers in cities use materials from the countryside to make products. Factory workers turn oil, cocoa beans, and cotton into gasoline, chocolate, and cloth. They also produce steel, paper, and cement. About 1 out of every 5 Nigerians has a **service job**. They work in banks, schools, hospitals, shops, and restaurants.

19

> **fun fact**
> A popular board game in Nigeria is *ayo*, also known as mancala. Players move seeds or stones around a board with rows of holes. Each village has its own rules.

Nigerians enjoy many different sports. Their favorite sport is soccer. Track-and-field, wrestling, and boxing are also popular. In traditional Hausa boxing, or *dambe*, only one hand is used to strike the opponent. This hand is called the spear. The other hand is called the shield. It is used to block.

When they want to relax, Nigerians watch television or see movies. Families and friends gather to listen to stories about the history of their town or village. Nigerians also love to keep up with the news. They listen to the radio or read the newspaper to find out what is happening in their country and around the world.

Did you know?
Nigerian girls often challenge their friends to dancing games where they try to match each other's steps.

plantains

Nigerians like spicy food. Most dishes are cooked in palm oil and seasoned with hot chili peppers. Many Nigerians start the day with *ogi*, a porridge made from grains. Others enjoy *garri*, or ground cassava. *Garri* can also be served with soups and stews for lunch or dinner. *Egusi* soup is a favorite food made with tomatoes, onions, vegetables, and meat or fish. It is thickened with ground-up melon seeds. *Fufu* is a mixture of cassava, yams, and **plantains**. *Puff-puffs* are a favorite snack. These small donuts are eaten during any part of the day.

fun fact

Kola nuts are used to flavor soft drinks in Nigeria and around the world. They are also offered to guests as a sign of friendship and welcome.

fufu

puff-puffs

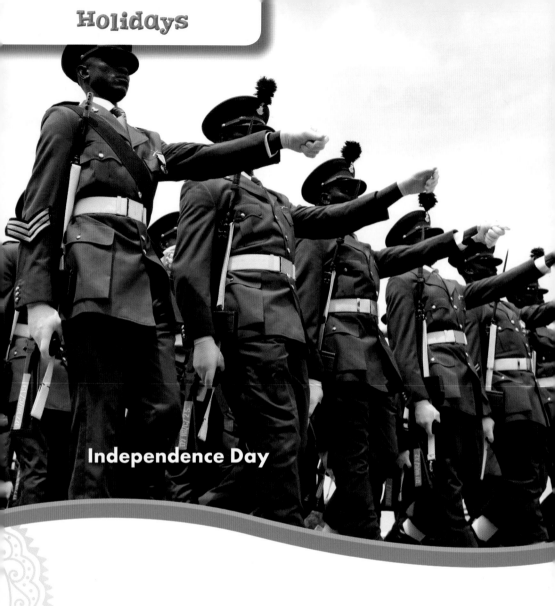

Independence Day

Nigerians celebrate many national holidays each year. On New Year's Day, some people stay home to pray and reflect on the past year. Others gather for lively parties with music, dancing, food, and fireworks. October 1 is Independence Day. People attend parades and special ceremonies. Nigeria's national colors, green and white, can be seen everywhere.

Muslims and Christians in Nigeria celebrate different religious holidays. Christian holidays include Christmas and Easter. On Christmas, Nigerian families gather together for large meals. Most Muslims in Nigeria observe **Ramadan**. Eid al-Fitr marks the end of Ramadan. It is celebrated with a *durbar* festival. This includes a colorful parade to honor leaders of the Muslim community.

fun fact

During a *durbar* parade, a Muslim leader and his guards ride through town on horseback. They all wear flashy costumes, and the guards carry swords or spears.

durbar

Argungu Fishing Festival

Every year, Nigerians and people from around the world look forward to the Argungu Fishing Festival. The four-day event began as a way to bring neighboring villages together in peace. During the first three days of the festival, people enjoy a motor rally, canoe races, and a fair. People dance to traditional music and watch many different sporting events.

Did you know?

Music adds to the excitement of the festival. Groups of drummers in canoes weave through the tangle of nets and people.

! fun fact

Whoever catches the biggest fish wins a car and 1 million naira. That is around 8,000 dollars!

The fishing competition happens on the last day. Thousands line up along the banks of the Sokoto River with nets to catch the fish. They bring large gourds to help them float. A gun is shot to signal the start of the contest. Everyone rushes into the river. They have one hour to try to catch the biggest fish they can. The Argungu Fishing Festival is a time for Nigerians to gather and celebrate their land, their culture, and each other.

Fast Facts About Nigeria

Nigeria's Flag

The Nigerian flag has three vertical stripes. The middle stripe is white, and there is a green stripe on each side. The green represents Nigeria's farmland and forests. The white stands for peace. This flag was adopted on October 1, 1960, the day Nigeria became an independent country.

Official Name: Federal Republic of Nigeria

Area: 356,669 square miles (923,768 square kilometers); Nigeria is the 32nd largest country in the world.

Capital City:	Abuja
Important Cities:	Lagos, Ibadan, Kano, Enugu, Port Harcourt
Population:	155,215,573 (July 2011)
Official Language:	English; Yoruba, Hausa, and Igbo are other common languages.
National Holiday:	Independence Day (October 1)
Religions:	Muslim (50%), Christian (40%), traditional beliefs (10%)
Major Industries:	farming, fishing, mining, services
Natural Resources:	oil, natural gas, coal, tin, iron ore, timber
Manufactured Products:	wood products, rubber, paper, leather, cement, clothing, fertilizers, chemicals, steel, food products, ceramics
Farm Products:	cocoa beans, peanuts, cotton, palm oil, corn, rice, sorghum, millet, cassava, taro, yams, rubber, cattle, sheep, goats, pigs, fish
Unit of Money:	naira; the naira is divided into 100 kobo.

Glossary

biomes—types of environments or habitats; deserts, savannahs, and tropical rain forests are examples of biomes.

continent—one of the seven main land areas on Earth; the continents are Africa, Antarctica, Asia, Australia, Europe, North America, and South America.

delta—the area around the mouth of a river

diversity—a variety of different cultures or groups of people

erosion—the slow wearing away of soil by water or wind

filter—to remove chemicals, salt, and other harmful materials from water

gulf—part of an ocean or sea that extends into land

mangrove forests—thick areas of trees and shrubs along coastline

natural resources—materials in the earth that are taken out and used to make products or fuel

plantains—tropical fruits that look like bananas; plantains are often eaten in Nigeria.

plateau—an area of flat, raised land

Ramadan—the ninth month of the Islamic calendar; Ramadan is a time when Muslims fast from sunrise to sunset.

savannahs—dry, grassy plains

service job—a job that performs a task for people or businesses

slums—areas of housing that are overcrowded and often dirty; many poor people in Nigeria live in slums.

tropical rain forests—thick, green forests that lie in the hot and wet areas near the equator; it rains about 200 days each year in many tropical rain forests.

tubers—underground stems or roots

wetlands—wet, spongy land; bogs, marshes, and swamps are wetlands.

To Learn More

AT THE LIBRARY

Giles, Bridget. *Nigeria*. Washington, D.C.: National Geographic, 2007.

Heinrichs, Ann. *Nigeria*. New York, N.Y.: Children's Press, 2010.

Levy, Patricia. *Nigeria*. New York, N.Y.: Benchmark Books, 2004.

ON THE WEB

Learning more about Nigeria is as easy as 1, 2, 3.

1. Go to www.factsurfer.com.

2. Enter "Nigeria" into the search box.

3. Click the "Surf" button and you will see a list of related Web sites.

With factsurfer.com, finding more information is just a click away.

Index

The images in this book are reproduced through the courtesy of: Friedrich Stark/Alamy, front cover; Maisei Raman, front cover (flag), p. 28; Juan Martinez, pp. 4-5, 5 (small), p. 11 (top); Oleg Znamenskiy, pp. 6, 11 (middle); National Geographic/Getty Images, p. 7; Jamikorn Sooktaramorn, pp. 8-9; Dariush M., pp. 10-11; Frans Lanting Studio/Alamy, p. 11 (bottom); Irene Abdou/Alamy, p. 12; Mark Shenley/Alamy, p. 14; Art Directors & TRIP/Alamy, p. 15; Chris Martin/Age Fotostock, pp. 16-17; Mark Shenley/Photolibrary, p. 18; Eye Ubiquitous/Photolibrary, pp. 19 (left), 26-27; Eric Miller/Photolibrary, p. 19 (right); Ahmad Faizal Yahya, p. 20; David Brimm, p. 20 (small); David Levenson/Alamy, p. 21; Peter Arnold, Inc./Alamy, p. 22; Anna Hoychuk, p. 23 (left); Robert Harding Images/Masterfile, p. 23 (right); Mirabelle Pictures, p. 23 (small); Sunday Alamba/AP Images, p. 24; AFP/Getty Images, p. 25; Getty Images, p. 27 (small); Jeff Banke, p. 29.